to David Feit-Pretzer, in celebration of 60 years of ministry as an organist

Fanfare Acclamation on "Majesty"

Based on the tune by Jack Hayford

Arr. by **Mark Thallander**
and **Bruce Wilkin**

Solo: Fanfare Trompette
Swell: Full to Reeds
Great: Full to Mixtures, Sw. to Gt., Ch. to Gt.
Choir: Full to Mixtures, Sw. to Ch.
Pedal: Full, Reeds 16, 8, 4, Sw. and Ch. to Ped.

BGK1086

17
22
Ch. f
27
So. fff
32
Gt. ff

37
Ch.
41
So.
fff
Gt.
ff
45
So.
fff
49
Add
Gt.
ff

53
So.
fff
Gt. ff
So.
fff
58
Gt. ff
62
66
Tutti
8va
rit.